Don't Tell Me
I Can't

An Ambitious

Homeschooler's Journey

Don't Tell Me I Can't

An Ambitious

Homeschooler's Journey

by Cole Summers

Don't Tell Me I Can't

Follow me!

Facebook @HomeschoolMBA

Twitter @thecolesummers

Table of Contents

To Mom, Dad, & Big Bro, thank
you for always helping and supporting
me through all my crazy projects.

To Willow, thank you so much for all
your help and encouragement with
getting this book done.

Introduction

"You're just a kid. You can't do that!"
~ Way too many adults

Online, in books, in schools, and in the news, my generation is constantly being told that our future sucks. It doesn't matter if it's climate change, water scarcity, food shortages, or other threats. The message is always that where we live may not stay livable. Even worse is that we're constantly told we can't do anything about it.

It's sad. I read about so many other kids my age, my peers, struggling with anxiety and depression. I can't relate to it, but I understand it. I hear and read where adults question "what's wrong with kids today?" What else do they expect when we're constantly told that our future is hopeless and we are hopeless?

I understand the concern about the future at least as well as anyone. I'm already living it. Human-damaged land down the road from my parent's house has created dust storms so thick that we could barely see a hundred feet out our front window. This was a reality of my life before I learned about the words "climate" or "environment," or what they meant. I don't have fears about the future because I'm told it will be bad. My fears are because I know the impact I already live with could get worse. And dust storms aren't the only, or even the worst, man-made environmental disaster I already have first-hand experience with.

But I'm not hopeless about it at all. Even though it is the literal, active, written plan by adults to make it worse, I have hope.

My first fourteen years on this earth have been different from most other kids. No one has taught me to be angry or upset about the disaster facing my future. I've never been told that it's a hopeless situation, or that I'm hopelessly at the mercy of what adults now choose to do. I've never spent a minute protesting to change the minds of adults who don't care what I think.

Like every other kid, I've had people tell me I can't do something because I'm "just a kid." This silly, adult idea that being young makes us incapable and incompetent has discouraged so many kids from learning what they're capable of and pursuing their dreams. But one of the biggest blessings in my life has been that every time I've heard that nonsense said to me, I can be sure of two things. First, it's never my parents that said it. Second, my parents will not only allow me to work to prove whoever said it wrong, but they encourage me to do so.

Why do adults do this to kids? What's the point in putting us down when we want to achieve more than what they *believe* we can do, while also saying how they hope their kids go further and do better than they ever did? I hear it in person and see it online all the time.

The first time I can remember facing this was when I was five. An older neighbor asked my mom to help them plant their garden. I tried to volunteer to do it, and they said I was too little. Too little for what? Too little to reach the ground with seeds that weigh less than a thumbnail?

I asked my parents if I could grow my own garden in our backyard. I had to prove I could do it. They said yes. That was it. No questions or directions. If I wanted to do it, I could. There weren't any limits on how big of a garden I could plant or what I wanted to grow.

I wish I had kept a record of my first garden. I dug out the grass and planted rows of corn, green beans, tomatoes, and carrots. I think I grew some zucchini too.

I wasn't too little. That neighbor had no reason to look down on me just because of my age. Thankfully, that garden incident grew in me a desire to keep proving people wrong and keep outperforming what adults thought I was capable of. And my parents have never failed to let me.

I haven't slowed down in my drive to outperform what others think I can do. I've proven many rumored legal restrictions on kids to be false. I started a small backyard farm that I've grown into a 350 acre ranch. And now I'm taking on the challenge of preserving a depleting aquifer without destroying the farm community that depends on it.

Little me. I was a natural country kid.

Chapter 1

Me Do It

Almost thirty years ago, an eighteen year old young man was injured during his military training. He didn't know it then, but just weeks before his nineteenth birthday, he became disabled for the rest of his life.

That's the start of my unschooling journey. That young man eventually became my dad, and it's his disability that gave my parents the sense of freedom to homeschool me and my brother. My dad hasn't been able to get a medical release to work in over 15 years. My mom can't work because my dad requires regular help. Since they're both home all the time, homeschooling wasn't hard to make happen.

I can't overstate the impact my dad's situation has had on my life. He would have never met my mom if he hadn't been injured, so I wouldn't even exist. When I was two, a surgery gone wrong put him in a wheelchair for the first time. My mom says that my reaction to that has shaped much of who I am today.

My dad waited seventeen months for another surgery that let him walk again. According to both of my parents, since I can't remember being two and three, I clung to my dad's side the entire time, eager to help him with anything he needed help with, and even most of what he didn't need help with. My dad likes to tease me that he still has most of the cartoon movie Bolt memorized. According to him, I was pretty insistent on watching it on repeat while being his helper.

Since he couldn't get to anything in the kitchen from his wheelchair, I always wanted to be the one to get my dad a drink or snack. When my mom would beat me to it, she says I would take it from her and say "me do it."

My parents have a video of me, not long before my third birthday, helping change a tire on their truck. It was a "me do it" moment, as they tell me. My mom was starting to pull tools out, but I insisted on taking over. The reason they videoed it was that every time I got a lug nut off, I would pull it out of the socket and toss it. They let me make that mistake. I don't know when I learned that I don't like chasing down lug nuts, but I stack them neatly now.

That's why my mom says it played such a big role in everything I've done since. Even after my dad had a surgery that let him walk short distances again, my "me do it" mindset was stuck.

My mom says letting me do these "grown up" things was pretty easy for her as long as she was confident I was safe. She wasn't allowed to do the same kind of things growing up, and says that she was totally unprepared to live as an adult when the time came. She doesn't want that for her kids.

It's harder for my dad, but not for any of the normal reasons adults tell me kids usually get told no. He openly talks with us about how emotionally hard it is to accept being disabled. Doing whatever he feels like he physically can is mental health care for him. Unfortunately, there isn't much he can physically do anymore.

Even when my dad would do what he could, he never stopped me from doing it along side him, and he never limited me to just being an errand boy that handed him tools. I was four the first time I disassembled a truck engine and helped rebuild it. I've been using saws, nail guns, and other tools for as long as I can remember.

When I see some of my friend's and their younger siblings, I see them wanting to do grown up stuff too. My dad's needs may have been a unique situation to me, but that drive to do grown up things isn't. They all have "me do it" desires too. The bigger difference with my family's life is that my parents often had to let me do some of these things or they wouldn't get done. Whereas with some of my friends and their siblings, I often hear their parents tell them they can't because they're "just a kid."

I've never accepted being told I can't do something. This isn't the same as things my parents decide not to allow me to do. By can't, I'm talking about not able to do. The minute an adult says I can't, all I want to do is prove them wrong. A big part of it was the feeling of accomplishment I got when I did "grown up" things. That's one part of my younger childhood I do remember. I was always proud of myself for doing grown up things.

A lot of people seem to think empowering a kid to do big things means having the money to pay for whatever the kid may want or need. Believe me, one thing disabled Veterans aren't is rich. I have total access to all of my parent's finances. I always have, which I guess is an unusual choice they made. They aren't pretending to be poor. When we had Christmases without presents, my brother and I knew to expect it because we knew what they could… and couldn't… afford. Christmas is always still wonderful because we spend time together playing board games and watching Christmas movies.

The empowering part is that they let me do it. Whatever "it" was. They encouraged me when I wanted to prove other adults wrong about what I could or couldn't do, and still do. My parent's never tell me I can't do something (unless it's illegal). Most of the time they do the exact opposite and tell me I can. Sometimes they believe in me more than I believe in myself.

That's empowering. Just being allowed to try gives me confidence. When my parents tell me I can do anything I put my mind to, they back it up. That's not something they say, but mean only when I'm older. They've let me do enough "grown up" things that I actually have experiences to write a biography about at fourteen years old.

It also makes me sad for other kids who don't get that chance, either because adults look down on them as "just kids," or because they don't get any say in how they spend any of their time. And that's why I decided to write this. To help other kids and parents see that we're capable of much more than most of us are allowed to do.

It may not work for every kid. We all have different situations and abilities. But most of the kids I know are capable of so much more than what adults will let them do. How are they to know what they can do if they're never allowed to try?

(left) My parents thought I might be hard to keep up with when I climbed on everything I could. I've never let anything stop me from what I wanted to do.

Having a little fun while learning to work on engines.

16

Chapter 2

Why Homeschool

I've heard lots of other adults ask my parents why they decided to homeschool. Sometimes you can just tell that they're genuinely curious. Other times they're defensive and say "what's wrong with public school?"

The reason that my parents chose to homeschool has interested me too. I've talked with them about it several times. I wanted to include it because, even though I wasn't there, like my dad's disability, it is a big part of my story.

The first time my parents ever considered homeschooling was when my mom was pregnant with me. They were living with her parents because my dad's health had cost him the last job he had. He was waiting for the VA to make a decision about how his disability had worsened and see if he might be able to work again.

Down the street from my grandparent's house was an elementary school. At the time, it was where my parents thought my brother and I would eventually go to school.

One afternoon, while they were sitting on the front porch, a group of several eight to ten year old kids came walking by from the school. My parents won't repeat what the kids were yelling, but said they were chanting something that my parents describe as disgusting, vulgar, and demeaning towards women.

"Maybe we should homeschool," my dad mentioned. My mom agreed. It wasn't an instant choice to homeschool. It was just an idea at first. One they started giving honest thought to.

At some point before I was born, my parents asked themselves how well public school had prepared them for their adult lives. They said they both weren't sure whether to laugh or cry at how unprepared they were for adult life.

When my parents first met, my dad was one of too many homeless disabled Veterans. He was getting training for a new job, where he met my aunt. That ultimately led to him meeting my mom. My mom was unemployed and living in her parent's basement, along with my aunt who only worked part time.

They thought about their family and friends who all went to public school too. Some were out on their own and had full time jobs. Some even owned their homes. But none of them were thriving in life. Several of them lost their homes and jobs during the Great Recession.

At best, they figured, public school prepared people to just barely get by when the economy was good. They also recognized that public school wasn't the only one raising them to be unprepared for life. Questioning their own parent's choices in raising them made them start questioning everything about their childhoods, in school and out.

The biggest thing to them was money. They were obviously broke and had spent their entire adult lives poor. School had taught them how to count money. Their parents taught them that the family budget was "none of your **** business." That was their financial education. They didn't know yet how to do any better, but they did decide right then that my brother and I would always have full access to their finances. If nothing else, we'd know what to expect things to cost when we became adults.

They asked themselves how much of what they learned in high school was required by any of the jobs they'd had or wanted. My dad had used algebra some, but not much. He otherwise agreed with my mom that most common jobs only needed skills they learned in elementary or middle school.

The rest of what the jobs needed were either college or trade school level skills, or something the companies trained employees to do.

While they were doing this, they looked into that school down the street. When they learned it was the lowest rated school in our state, the idea of homeschooling felt even more appealing.

Once the VA finished my dad's review, they found him to be 100% disabled and unable to work anymore. Neither of my parents were surprised by the decision. That's when homeschooling went from being an idea they liked to something they thought they could do.

It wasn't that my parents thought they would do a better job than public school. They were just confident they couldn't do any worse. It wasn't because they thought teachers were bad at what they do. It was that the things they taught weren't exactly useful to their lives as adults.

Every adult I know has admitted that studying things like old poetry has never helped them pay their mortgage.

My parents weren't prepared to be teachers. They knew all the basic skills we would need for elementary and middle school. That meant they had seven years to learn more or refresh what they learned in high school if they needed to. If teachers could learn it in four years of college, they could learn it in seven years on their own.

With my dad's disability income increased, my parents were eager to get back out on their own again. They started looking at houses in the city, but they never liked anything they found that they could afford. They considered buying land and building, but realized that was more than they could do themselves.

One of them eventually had the idea to search online for whatever was the cheapest house in our entire state. Since my dad's income wasn't from a job that he had, that gave them the freedom to live anywhere they wanted. That cheap house was a foreclosure out in the middle of nowhere farm country. An old doublewide trailer on an old, trashed out, five acre homestead. They bought it.

This presented them with a new situation. The elementary school here was (and still is) one of the highest rated in the state. So is the local high school. It made them feel better that they had a Plan B if homeschooling didn't work out, so they decided to give it a try.

Their choice to move to a rural area and homeschool me was the foundation for everything I've done in my life so far, and everything I plan to do with my future.

But there was a bigger lesson for me in learning the background of why my parents chose to homeschool in the first place. It wasn't an intentional thought process, even though it worked out that way. And at the end of it, they realized their odds of preparing my brother and I at least as well as public school would were good. There was a chance we would do better. And they had a backup plan if they were wrong. This is something I think about when I look at my future plans and choices I have to make, except that I do go through an intentional thought process.

One of my favorite things to do is cook. My friend and I were making cookies together.

Since we don't have neighborhoods, my parents would bury candy in bags & give us and our friends treasure maps. It was our Trick-or-Treasure Hunt every Halloween. This was an early challenge in life that I loved.

Chapter 3

Unschooling Begins

"Daddy, how do people get rich?"

I asked that question when I was six years old. I didn't understand much about money or finances yet, but I knew we weren't rich. I knew there were things we didn't have because we couldn't afford them.

My dad was dismissive and told me "I wouldn't know. Go watch videos on YouTube about Warren Buffett or something." So I did.

My dad being dismissive wasn't normal for him. He's never like that with my brother and I unless he's got something really important on his mind or something is really bothering him. It wasn't him being like "yeah, shut up and go away."

The start of my unschooling came at the time that the big scandal about VA healthcare became national news. The government created the Choice Card program, and suddenly my dad started getting approval for care for everything. He had nine surgeries in eighteen months. He would have had more but, as he says, he was tired of counting down from ten.

My dad now says it's a good thing he was so focused on his medical care. That if he had really paid attention to me he probably would have unintentionally misled me about how he thought things worked, and I would have kept on doing homeschool that mostly copied public school.

I responded to all these surgeries the same way I had when I was two. I didn't quite cling to his side, but I stayed constantly close by to help with anything that he needed. Except this time, instead of watching Bolt on repeat, I was watching video after video of Warren Buffett and other famous business leaders. My dad got into watching it with me.

We streamed endless hours of videos of interviews, speeches, and documentaries on several of the biggest, most successful names in business. They all freely share and teach how they achieved what they had, what choices they made, why they made their choices, and what lessons they learned along the way.

Before this, my parents did homeschool the "normal" way. They wanted me following a curriculum and mostly doing things the same way as public school. I argued at some point that I was learning more watching these videos than the "class work," and fortunately, they allowed me to continue. I think part of it was that they didn't want to fight me on it with all the surgeries he was having. We didn't know then that "unschooling" was a thing. It was just how my education worked out.

The only requirement they put on me with it was that I had to practice my reading. But even with that, reading articles about businesses and business leaders was fine. As long as I was reading, they didn't try to force what I read.

At six years old I was almost fully in control of everything I was learning. It probably helped that we don't have much to distract me into other things. We don't own any video games at all. My parents never got into them much, and as I said, they're poor. I'm probably one of the only fourteen year olds in America that's never played a video game.

I don't remember the exact video I started with, but I remember that it was one where Mr. Buffett talked about his decision making process. I don't know why I found it so interesting as a six year old, but I did. Maybe because of how simple it is. Mr. Buffett's main goal isn't in trying to make great choices in his investments. He just tries to avoid making bad choices.

He gives the example of being a baseball player up at bat. But in his example, the baseball player isn't limited to just three pitches to try to hit the ball. Instead, the baseball player can wait through all the pitches he wants to wait through until he gets just the right pitch. The pitch he's confident he can hit a home run off of. He gets to ignore, or say no to, every pitch that's outside his comfort zone. While waiting, he's saving his energy to smash that perfect pitch that is right in his comfort zone.

This doesn't mean the baseball player will have a perfect batting average. He'll have bad days and other things that might mess him up. But odds are pretty good he'd have one of the best batting averages ever.

I liked the idea of making mostly good choices. I understood it just fine. In investments, and in life, the comfort zone of pitches is what Mr. Buffett calls our "circle of competence." I didn't understand the word competence at the time, but he explained that too. It's simply whatever we've spent significant time studying or doing, so that we have strong and trustworthy knowledge about it.

Any time I hear an adult say something about "how to think, not what to think," I ask what they mean by that. What do they mean by how to think. The answer is the same every single time. "Just think for yourself." As good as it is to think for yourself, I hate that answer. It's the only "how" question no one ever answers with an actual method or process.

That's what stands out to me the most about studying what all these rich business founders and leaders teach. Every one of them has a process for their thoughts and choices, and they're mostly all the same.

Some adults have tried telling me that teaching a process of how to think is still teaching what to think. That a process means everyone reaches the same conclusion. It doesn't. The process is about finding whatever is best for you. Helping you avoid problems and make better decisions for your circumstances.

A lot of adults also say there isn't a process. It's just something we all have to figure out for ourselves. I've seen too many YouTube videos with the theme of "What was that idiot thinking?" to accept that answer. People making stupid choices has created billion dollar industries, and the ones getting rich off it all have methods to how they think.

My favorite teacher I'll never meet is Charlie Munger. He's Warren Buffett's long-time partner at Berkshire Hathaway, and best friend. My favorite lesson from Mr. Munger is a speech he gave at Harvard called The Path to Misery. His second item for a path to misery is to learn as much as possible from our own experience, ignoring what we can learn from other's experience.

"But experience is the best teacher." Is it? Really? I don't want to learn by my own experience that borrowing tens of thousands of dollars from the government to go to college turns into a life-long debt trap for many people. I don't want to learn by my own experience that the VA does a crappy job of meeting disabled Veteran's needs. My dad learned that the hard way, so I shouldn't have to. There are so many things I don't want to ever learn by my own experience because they reliably create misery and hardship.

Learning by other's experience is more than just learning what to avoid. It's also about getting a head start on our achievements by learning what worked well for others. A simple example is cooking. We can try throwing random ingredients together and hope it isn't disgusting, or we can start with a recipe and tweak it to our tastes or needs. Starting with a recipe saves us time and money to let us reach the goal faster.

Cooking may be an easy example, but the same idea applies to a lot of things. I've used it to save time setting up businesses, on my farming, planning for taxes, and all kinds of things. It's easier to be successful if you start by building on other's successes, and that requires learning from their experiences.

I did learn a lot about business and finance from studying these people. But the valuable lesson was having mental processes to improve my odds of making good choices for my life and my goals.

Learning to use mental tools like the 80/20 Principle and opportunity cost have helped me with everything I've done since then. Applying the process of elimination to daily life makes us give real thought to the best use of our time. Using First Principles to break down things we want to do or have to its most basic parts helps to achieve goals that people say we "can't" do. That's what Elon Musk and his team used, upending decades of rocket science that said reusable rockets are impossible.

That's what the first year of my unschooling journey was. My first grade year was learning, along with my dad, how to think. It was all new to him too. He would often stop our lessons to tell me about times in his life he would have done something totally different if anyone had taught this to him.

I was learning my math and reading skills along the way because those were part of what I wanted to learn. I don't like math. Not school book math. It's boring. Learning it on the side as it was needed by other things I wanted to learn made a big difference.

Even though I was studying Warren Buffett, Charlie Munger, and Elon Musk, I still spent more time playing than anything else.

I love all my animals. We've never not had cats around the farm.

Chapter 4

My First Business

During this time, I learned how to calculate net worth with my dad. It was as new to him as it was me. We spent time going through all my parent's finances together and doing the math. I still feel bad for my dad when he discovered he had a negative net worth. He's admitted since then that he felt like a total failure when he saw negative $70,000 as his net worth, but I could see it on his face as soon as he saw the number.

I knew from my studies that the best way to build wealth is to own something and work to make it more valuable. Bill Gates bought and created software and worked insane hours to make his software company more valuable. Warren Buffett bought Berkshire Hathaway and worked to make it more valuable. Elon Musk and Peter Thiel created PayPal and worked insane hours to make it more valuable. It's the same story, over and over. Apple, Walmart, Tesla, Space-X, Amazon, Google. The famous names behind every one either created or bought something and worked tirelessly, along with teams they put together, to make it more valuable.

Some people like jumping to criticize some of these businesses, especially for how some workers get treated or paid. I'm not going into that, other than to point out that it doesn't change the process. Buying or creating something and working to make it more valuable is the same, even in companies that are employee-owned. The only change is in how the results get shared. The process stays the same.

Billionaires are the most famous, but it's the same process house flippers do too. My dad has a friend that buys and fixes up classic cars, making them more valuable. Construction companies do it when they buy land and build a house on it. Farmers do it when they improve their soil. Chefs make food and seasonings more valuable by how they put them together.

This works for us as people too, not just businesses. When we learn new-to-us knowledge and skills that are useful, it usually increases our value to the world around us.

I knew my parents would say yes when I asked to start my first business at age seven. My parents raised rabbits for meat in our backyard to help provide healthy food they could afford. It was my only option. When you live on a dirt road and only have one neighbor within a mile, a lemonade stand or yard cutting isn't going to make any money.

I did the research online to find that there is a profitable market for rabbit meat. My dad helped me find a meat processor and a way to get the rabbits there. My parents gave me my first five rabbits and let me use a run down old barn in their backyard. Along with my brother, I was in business as a rabbit farmer. My profit was $4 per rabbit, on average, and rabbits are kind of famous for reproducing quickly.

I make it sound quick and easy, but it wasn't. First off, that old barn was a disaster. My parents managed to get some old photos of their house from back when it was a running farm in 1953. That barn didn't look new even in those photos.

With my mom and brother's help, we deconstructed some other, unused outbuildings to salvage some wood. My dad helped me buy a little bit of new lumber too. It took us most of the summer when I was seven to clean up and repair that old barn to make it usable. It's still a crappy old building I should have just replaced years ago, but it's still holding up.

One experience from repairing that barn I won't ever forget is the first time I ever got sprayed by a skunk. I wanted to take a small break from the barn itself and work on a side project we were going to do around it. The area around the barn grew no plants at all. It was just barren desert with old farm trash scattered about. We were going to constantly spread the rabbit poop around and collect seeds to plant there.

One piece of trash was a part of an eight-inch irrigation pipe sticking out of a small sand dune that had built up on an old fence. I walked up to it, bent down to look inside, and got nailed by skunk spray. It wasn't quite as bad of an experience as the first time I had to pay taxes, or any time I've paid taxes, but it wasn't fun.

We made a bunch of noise around the pipe and waited for the skunk to find itself a new home, then pulled the pipe out.

The best part of that is how our attempt to create usable soil turned out. My brother and I used a wheelbarrow at least once a month to haul the poop out and spread it around. There's so much sagebrush, salt brush, and crested wheat grass growing there now that it's hard to walk through.

One thing I see in the news a lot is articles that ramble on and on about "self-made" riches. It's a load of crap, and the people they're writing about all admit that it is. Warren Buffett is probably the closest to "self-made" that there is and he is always giving credit to the people that taught him how to invest, the people that first trusted him and gave him a chance to invest their money, and all the people he's worked with and learned from all these years.

The start of every success story is a team. The people who have the idea, put together the teams, and take the biggest risks to make it work get most of the wealth and fame, but none of them did it alone.

I've been able to achieve a lot more than most kids my age, and there is absolutely no way I could have done it on my own. My family doesn't have much money to contribute, but they've been the team helping me with their time on every crazy project I take on. My mom and brother have done more hours of labor than we can count. My dad helps drive me places and saves me so much time in helping me research and find the best books to learn from. I am not and never will be "self-made," and I hope no one ever calls me that.

In just one of the ways I'm not "self-made," was in how I setup my business. I was just going to be a sole-proprietor, and maybe setup an LLC later if it was working out. It was my dad's idea to treat my tiny start of a rabbit farm like I was doing a Silicon Valley tech startup. It wasn't about ambition or where we thought I could take the business. It was a purely educational idea to learn and know all the legal requirements and formalities of running a corporation. But that idea helped me learn more that has added to some of my success since.

At seven years old I was the majority shareholder in a corporation that owned five breeding rabbits and several dozen young rabbits that would soon become food in restaurants. I was very proud of myself. I kept most of the girl rabbits (does) and a few of the boys (bucks) so I could grow my business. My company was earning almost a thousand dollars a month by the time I turned eight. Then a disaster happened.

I can't legally say what the disaster was, but something beyond my control killed every rabbit I had. Even though they were meant to become food, I tried hard to make sure my rabbits had happy and healthy lives. When they started getting sick and dying, it devastated me. It devastated my whole family. We all cried, not because of the business impact, but because we couldn't stand seeing animals suffer.

Once we learned what was happening, it was too late. The only choice we had was to end their suffering as quick and painlessly as we could. A neighbor with a big hay and cattle farm was nice enough to help me and bring over a tractor to dig a big hole in the ground to bury them.

The insurance settlement I got wasn't a bright side to the disaster. I spent a few months debating whether I even wanted to restart my farm or not. My parents did nothing but comfort me. They never tried to push me one way or another. Whatever I chose to do, I knew I had their support.

There's something else very important that my parents have never done. Even though they're poor and I was making some good money, my parents never once took a dime from me. They don't "borrow" from me or tell me how to spend any of it. When they had a personal financial disaster in 2021, they wouldn't accept money from me to help unless it was me paying a fair value to buy something from them.

Trusting that I could keep what I earned mattered a lot to my choices. They would help me do research and planning so I could have some idea what the results of my choices would be. But they were my choices to make. I could restart my farm. I could start an entirely new business. I could choose to save it all and go to public school. I could choose to blow it on toys and candy. I don't think I would have kept going if my parents hadn't done this.

When I was ready and I did make my choice, Charlie Munger's Path to Misery lesson was a big influence. Mr. Munger's third prescription to guarantee a life of misery is to go down and stay down when life gets hard. I chose to get back up. I not only restarted my farm, but I started another business too.

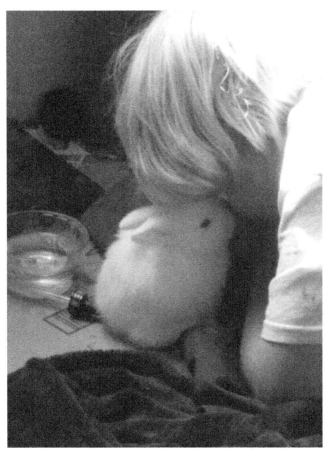

I brought some of the first sick rabbits to live in my bedroom
so I could take good care of them. Age 8.

50

Chapter 5

That Ain't So

I'm going to paraphrase a quote that gets attributed to Mark Twain.

"It ain't what you don't know that holds your kids back, it's what you think you know that just ain't so."

When I was eight, while I was temporarily out of business, an older neighbor came to ask my dad for help fixing his pickup. My dad had fallen recently, hurt his back, and couldn't help. I saw an opportunity and jumped at it.

Our neighbor needed the valves on his cylinder heads replaced. It was a job I knew how to do because my parents never told me I can't do things. With some supervision and guidance, I've done most of the auto maintenance and repairs for my family since I was six, and done almost all of it on my own since I was twelve.

Our neighbor had an old, beat-up, non-running, 1976 Chevy 4x4 pickup in his backyard that I day dreamed about every time we drove past his house. I offered to do the valve job on the truck he used in exchange for the pickup in his backyard. He agreed, but told me he was pretty sure I couldn't have the truck in my name until I was eighteen.

I hear and read this "common knowledge" in person and online a lot. Kid's can't own this, kid's can't do that. Guess what? I've had a 1976 Chevy 4x4 pickup titled in my own name, and only my name, since I was eight years old. I can't drive it, which is okay since I still haven't put a new engine in it yet. I can't have insurance in my own name yet either. But I can and do own that pickup.

I still have people tell me that kids can't actually own a business either. Not a legitimate business entity like a corporation or LLC. It's supposedly illegal. The last time I researched it there were only seven states where this was true. Here's a fun tip about businesses. They don't have to be created in the state where you live. If you live in a state with a stupid law designed to hold kids back in life, setup your business in a better state. That's a common business practice.

Kids can own businesses. We can even be the only owner of the business. The business does have to have an adult officer that can sign legal documents, but that adult doesn't have to be an owner. Also, banking laws require that an adult be on the bank account of the company. But with proper identification, the kid can have full, equal control over the money with the adult. I've been writing and signing checks for years, perfectly legal.

I hired a business attorney when I was ten and he's helped me learn more about what legal "can't" things apply to kids. Every state may be a little different, but most of the limits are that contracts signed by kids might not be enforceable. I still work with that lawyer, but he won't do as I ask him to without one of my parents agreeing. That's because he would have a hard time requiring me to pay him if I decided to back out of the agreement.

It's "common knowledge" that kids can't own property either. It depends on state (and maybe local) laws, but I found out that's not true where I live either. I can own property. My first property was my ninth birthday present to myself.

A few miles from my parent's house is a 350 acre property that had been for sale for over seven years. The big, old-money farmers didn't want it because of how much work it would take to make it a usable hayfield. It doesn't have much grass, being covered mostly in sagebrush, so it isn't useful for sheep or cattle either.

My dad likes to say that I don't just think outside the box, but that I rip up every box that I can get my hands on.

I wanted to raise meat goats on that property. Something no one else around here raises. There's a few people with some pet milk goats, but no one ranching meat goats.

With my parent's help (because of the contract laws) I made an offer that the real estate agent said was a waste of time. He said I "can't" buy it that cheap because the seller had turned down offers in the past that were more than double the $130 per acre that I offered. The next morning the agent called back and said that three years of no offers at all must have worn them down. I got the ranch.

Don't ever take "can't" as the answer unless you've verified that it is against the law or against the laws of physics. People told me I can't legally own property. The agent said I can't buy it for such a cheap price. They were wrong.

If my parents and I listened to the rumors by people who *think* they know what they're talking about, my life would be very different. It turns out that a lot of people think they know things that just ain't so.

8 year old me standing proudly by my beat up old 1976
Chevy 4x4 that I earned in trade with a neighbor.

Taking off the tire so I could put new shocks on the family
Suburban. Age 8.

Chapter 6

Looking for Luck

Being able to buy my ranch stirred my interest in property. I wanted to learn more. Thankfully, learning about real estate isn't much harder than reading books and doing some good online searches.

When I restarted my farm, I also restructured my company. I made my corporation a holding company, started an LLC that my holding company owns to be the farm operating company, and started another LLC for property investments. There are a lot of reasons to do this, but protecting my assets is the main reason. I didn't want someone getting hurt on a property and being able to get anything from my farm.

Like many places nowadays, the property records here are online. I can pull up forty years of title history on almost every parcel in the county with just a few clicks. One property I found was a house in the city. When my dad drove me over to look at it we could tell it had obviously been abandoned for years and was a total mess. This house had what's called a "lawyer's lien" against it, and it was five years behind on property taxes.

Being five years behind on property taxes meant it was about to get auctioned off by the county in a few months. The lawyer's lien meant the lawyer was owed money from the house. The owner had to pay the lien or the lawyer would get paid first if the house got sold.

I showed my dad and he thought there was no way the lawyer would sell a lien that was guaranteed to get paid in a few months. I wanted to try anyways. The worst that could happen was getting told no.

That lawyer wasn't paying any attention to that house or lien at all. He had forgotten about it!

After the phone call I wished I had offered him less. The lawyer sold me the lien for half of what he was owed as soon as I offered it.

A few weeks later the son of the lady the lawyer did the work for (she had died) found a buyer for his mom's house, and I got paid the full amount owed on the lien, doubling my money.

I had learned never to accept "can't" as an answer unless I verified a reason. So I wasn't about to let a "probably not" stop me. It was unlikely the lawyer was going to agree to sell it. Even more unlikely that he would have forgotten it. So what. The worst thing that can happen when someone says "no" is you move on.

Another property that I got a yes to was from a widow that didn't want her late husband's weekend camping land anymore. She was tired of paying taxes on it and couldn't understand why anyone would want desert sagebrush land in the middle of nowhere, so she offered it to me for

$100 per acre. My deal for her twenty acres turned out way better for me than I could have dreamed.

When I first bought my ranch it had a water well already on it. That was part of why I wanted it. There is an old abandoned house on it too, but it's so torn up and run down it can't be fixed anymore.

There had been about twelve feet of water at the bottom of the well when I bought it. I did a search online and read about lowering a string with weight at the bottom down the hole, and then measuring how much of the string was wet when I pulled it back up. Twelve feet isn't much, but I didn't need much to water my goats.

When the time came for me to install the solar well pump I bought, I got no water out of my well. It was dry. I didn't yet know how expensive new water wells were, but I knew it was more than I had.

The well driller here is a really cool guy. He's a skinny, old cowboy with a big handlebar mustache. I don't see him a lot, but every time I do he cheers me on for ignoring people who say what I can't do.

I know I sighed and dropped my head when he told us it was going to be twenty-thousand dollars for a new well. I didn't have to tell him I didn't have it, and he knew my parents didn't.

"Got any property you'd be willing to trade me?" he asked. I wanted to jump up and down like a kid excited to get a new toy. I think I kind of did. He took the twenty acres I bought off the widow as a full trade for a new well.

I've had friends and extended family tell me I just get lucky easily. Luck is kind of funny in how it works. A lot of the time, when we have bad luck, it's something that just happened. My dad getting injured in the military is an easy example of that. He never went to war or did anything all that risky. It was a slip and fall while doing running drills, similar to the running drills he had done playing football when he was in school. He hit a spot where the grass happened to be wet and that was it. My great-grandmother described it, saying it looked like skin was the only thing keeping his foot attached.

Accidents happen. It's bad luck. Sometimes bad luck is really bad consequences of bad choices. If you get in a wreck while texting on the phone, that might be bad luck for another person you hit, but it's a bad consequence for you. But bad luck is real and sometimes we can't help it. That was the case with my rabbits that died.

I think this is why some people expect good luck to work the same way. Bad luck sometimes just falls in our laps no matter what we do, so they expect good luck to do that too.

From everything I've read and grown ups I've talked to, good luck almost never works like bad luck. Good luck requires us to do something on purpose to earn it. We either have to make sure we're ready to use it when it does come, or go out looking for it.

It was good luck that my dad was busy dealing with stuff to get his surgeries done, but it wasn't good luck that I took him seriously and watched my first Warren Buffett video. That was a choice. Something I did on purpose.

It was good luck that my parents already raised rabbits for meat and had a crappy old barn in their back yard. But I had to work hard to fix that barn up. I had to ask for my first rabbits to get started.

I spent months studying real estate and weeks studying local properties when I was nine years old. I took the risk of getting told no on a few dozen different properties. Only three said yes.

The things I just got lucky on was being born to parents who would eventually decide to homeschool, and let me turn that into unschooling. I was lucky to be born in a country where a poor kid born to poor, disabled parents can actually go looking for opportunities (my mom is partially blind and can't see well enough to drive). My biggest good luck was that my parents let "me do it," when I wanted to, even though I was "just a kid."

That third property I got told yes to, that I got lucky on after months of searching for the owner, turned into one of my biggest achievements.

Drilling the first fence post hole on my ranch.

Chapter 7

My First House

The timing wasn't on purpose. I had to hire a lawyer and the paperwork took a few months. My dad got openly exhausted at the legal mess it was. But eventually, for my tenth birthday, I bought a house. It cost me right at $10,000 after everything was done.

This wasn't some fancy, nice house in the city. I couldn't afford anything like that. About seven miles from my parent's house, in the middle of absolute nowhere, sat this run down old shack that was about to go on the tax auction. Half the roof was missing. A window was broken. A storage shed in the yard had collapsed. The trees looked awful. And that's just the outside. I had no way to see the inside yet.

When my dad and I found the owner, her first question was if I planned to tear it down or not. Apparently the only reason she hadn't sold it was because every possible buyer told her they would tear it down. Her father had built that little house himself. She couldn't afford to keep it up or repair it, but she wasn't going to sell it for it to be destroyed.

She agreed to sell it to me in exchange for paying for her trip to come get her dad's keepsakes out of it, plus I had to pay the back due taxes.

A 700 square foot, two bedroom house was all mine. Not that I could move into it, or wanted to, but it was totally unlivable. There was no floor. Part of the ceiling had caved in. Half the walls needed major drywall repair. I think that's the first time my dad worried I was in over my head. I probably was, but a local rancher that wanted that house so he could tear it down and build a new one unintentionally motivated me.

"You're just a kid. What you should do is sell it to me and double your money." The way he said it was obvious he was talking down to me. If he had been nice about it I would have been tempted to take his offer. I couldn't because I promised her I would fix it up. But I probably would have been tempted. As my dad and I were driving back home was the first time I said he (the rancher) can "kiss my butt, get out of my way, and watch me!" He didn't think a kid could fix up a old, run down house. I had to prove him wrong.

There is no way I could have ever done this project without one of the greatest educational tools ever created. YouTube. I learned plumbing, roofing, flooring, cabinet making, painting, and electrical work. I learned them all, and did them all.

With my mom and brother's help, it took me almost two years to fix up that old house. I had to stop because I ran out of money several times. I took a break to put up the first mile of fencing on my ranch. The house really did slow me down and distract me from my farm and ranch a lot, but I don't regret it.

When it came time to do the electrical work, like replacing all the wall outlets, ceiling fans, and light fixtures, was the one time my dad didn't let me make the choice myself. I had hired out the drywall work already. One limit of being a kid is being small. Drywall is big, kind of heavy, and awkward. But my dad was concerned about safety and made me hire help for the electrical work too.

Joey, my electrician, was awesome. I told him I wanted to do the work myself, and with my dad's permission, he taught me how to do it myself, safely. He stayed the whole time, and he was the one handing me tools.

Joey was amazed that a kid owned that house and was doing so much of the work. He said so over and over. He had just had his first kid and said it made him think he might homeschool his kid too. Like our well driller, he kept encouraging me to do whatever I'm capable of and ignore anyone who tells me I can't.

As we got close to finishing the electrical work, he asked me what I was doing with the kitchen. Using some of my dad's old tools that he can't use anymore, and a few that I bought for myself, I was almost finished building brand new, custom cabinets.

I didn't buy the pre-made cabinets that hardware stores sell. I bought full sheets of plywood and made the cabinets from scratch. I didn't have much of a choice. The way the wall and windows were built, none of the pre-made cabinets would fit. I ended up making a stained, epoxy coated wood counter top too, but my mom insisted on doing the epoxy. She didn't want me breathing any of the fumes.

Joey asked me to call him when I was ready to install the cabinets. He kept saying he was so excited to see a kid doing the work that he just wanted to help. And he did. Joey met my family there with me and we all worked until almost two in the morning. Even my dad found a way to help with some sanding and a few other things he could reach from his wheelchair. I was the reason we went that late. My parents were less than thrilled, but I didn't want to quit.

Most of that day while we worked together, Joey was asking me all kinds of questions about how I homeschool. At first he thought that I did regular school subjects, and then loads of business learning as extras.

He saw something I had written down as a note to myself and said "Dude, you better work on that spelling if you're going to get a good job one day." I asked if he had a problem reading it and he said "no. But important papers need the spelling to be right."

I explained that important papers would all be typed and spellcheck would fix most of it. Plus, everybody in that room had talk-to-type in their back pockets. It wasn't that I thought spelling was useless or unimportant. I just didn't think it was important enough to spend extra time being perfect on it instead of growing my business. My spelling got my point across and I could get better as I needed to.

Joey sighed and looked around. "I can't argue with that," he said. He commented about him being the one working for an eleven year old and said it was making him question a lot of what he thought he knew.

He wanted to understand how I studied math too. A lot of it was the same. At first I just learned what math I needed as I needed it. But the more I did the more I realized that memorizing basic, common math problems was very helpful in a lot of things. But I still learn math processes as I need them. The internet makes it so quick and easy to find what I need that I don't waste time learning stuff I might not ever use.

Adults often come back with "well what if the internet isn't around to help you anymore?" I wonder if they even realize that if the internet disappears, we don't have a society left to need complex math and perfect spelling in. Some people don't like it (I don't), but without the internet we don't having banking, phones, or supply chains anymore. If the internet dies, cramming algebra won't be my biggest priority.

Working with Joey was one of my two favorite parts of fixing up that old house. It meant a lot to me to have an adult, besides my parents, believe in me. My other favorite part was the rancher telling me I did a good job afterwards.

One other big moment for me during that project was when one of my public school friends came to help me one weekend. I bought myself a router and was making all my own door and window trim and baseboards.

This was maybe a month before my twelfth birthday, and it was the first time I learned that public school kids didn't get to do the same things I was doing. Before that, I always thought public school kids got to do fun stuff in school, plus all the same kinds of things I was doing too. I never put it together that there was no way they could spend so much time in school and get to do what I was doing.

When everything else was done with the house, I still had one big problem I couldn't solve. The well was just as dry as my bank account. A recurring problem I've had to deal with that motivates my future goals.

Installing new flooring in my house. Age 11.

I started with sheets of plywood and made new custom
cabinets and the counter top myself. Age 12.

Doing my own shopping at the hardware store to buy
supplies for my house.

Chapter 8

Life Changing Moments

I don't know what it was about my birthdays there for a few years, but it almost seemed like a habit to do something huge for them. After buying a ranch for my ninth birthday, and a house for my tenth, I bought my first tractor for my eleventh birthday.

That's why I couldn't afford a new well at the house. I didn't buy a small yard tractor, or even a small utility tractor. I went for a series two John Deere with a front loader, forklift attachment, backhoe, disc harrow, and some other tools. It's still the most expensive thing I've ever bought, but it was so worth it!

While I was working to save up more money to get back to fixing up my house, I spent the summer while I was eleven treating my ranch like a real job. I had set up a plan to divide my ranch into four paddocks that are eighty acres each, and put a water trough and holding pen in the middle of the four paddocks. My goats could graze each paddock for three months in a rotation. The well, that I didn't know yet was going dry, was half a mile from where I needed my water trough.

Every morning that summer, I got up, did my morning exercise, then jumped up on my tractor to drive to work. I got a lot of experience running my backhoe. I also learned how to deal with busted hydraulic lines and warranty repairs.

It wasn't exactly an eventful summer. Drive down the road, dig all day, drive home. One of my parents would often come down to sit with me during breaks or bring me snacks and drinks. I carved out a little spot under a huge bush to sit and relax in the shade when I wanted to take breaks. Sometimes those breaks might have gone a little too long, but it was nice to sit and enjoy the quiet while looking across my land to the mountains.

There were two valuable things I learned that year. The first came while I was digging the half-mile long, three foot deep trench for a water line. Keep sharp backhoe teeth! I didn't know then that if I had kept sharp teeth on my backhoe, I would have finished that job in half the time or less. Won't make that mistake again. The other lesson came later, after I found out my well was dry.

An expensive hole in the ground wasn't the most valuable part of getting my new water well. Education was. I said the well driller was a cool guy, and he really is. He made me stay a safe distance from the drilling rig, but he taught me a lot about how the machine works, the clay he uses, the pipe. And even that wasn't the most valuable part.

What our well driller taught me that fall, right after my twelfth birthday (yes, the well was basically another big birthday present), was how the water table worked where I live. Every spring, when the hay farmers turn on their irrigation systems, the water table drops about thirty feet. Later, in the fall, the water table comes back up about twenty-four to twenty-seven feet. So the water table is dropping three to six feet every year. This was going to become life-changing knowledge for me.

When I measured the well when I was buying my ranch, I measured late in the fall. Had I known better and measured it in the summer, it would have been dry. And in the two years since I measured it, extreme drought led to two years of the water table dropping six feet both years. That was some genuine bad luck.

I asked our well driller about working out a deal on my house, suggesting he could have all the rent money until the well was paid for. He said he might work something out once I could afford at least half the well in cash. I knew that would take a while.

Once I had my new, 250 foot deep hole in the ground, the first paddock on my ranch was ready for my goats. I relaxed some that winter once the last repairs on my house were finished, and started making plans for the next year.

I already knew I'd spend most of the next year building another four miles of fencing to finish enclosing my ranch and dividing up the paddocks.

As spring came around, our world got turned upside down. And by "our," I mean every human on earth. That's when covid started. Since all of my rabbits ended up on the tables of restaurants in California, I lost all my sales.

2020 wasn't quite as bad on my family as it was on a lot of other people. My dad's Dr called and was clear that my dad had to be very careful. A common side effect of being disabled and sitting or laying down most of the time is the risk of blood clots. In my dad's case, we've been lucky that he's survived each time, but he's had several blood clots in his lungs over the years. Since his lungs are already damaged from blood clots, he was extreme high risk.

The bright side of the plan to fence off my ranch is that we weren't going to be around anyone else much that year anyway. Building four miles of fence on a rural ranch has some built-in social distancing that comes with it. My whole family was set to spend most of that year on my ranch, so it worked out fine.

Losing all sales was pretty scary. I wasn't going to get an insurance settlement this time. No one knew at the time how long it would all last. Ultimately, I decided to sell my house. I could see that I was going to have a hard time saving up for another new well with no sales. Without a working well, I had to sell it for almost half of what it would have sold for with a working well. Buyers couldn't get a mortgage without running water. I still ended up more than doubling my money on it, so I can't complain.

I wasn't forgetting Charlie Munger's lesson. I was getting knocked down again, but I moved quick to be ready to get back up. I took what I got from the sale of the house and started investing into my farm. I bought my first batch of heritage turkeys so I could expand into pasture raised turkey meat, and I bought everything I would need to be able to process them.

The first year of raising turkeys was just raising what I bought from baby poults up into my first breeding flock. Bourbon Red turkeys are beautiful birds to raise. They've proven to be pretty easy to raise too. And they taste so much better than the factory farmed, unnatural franken birds at the store!

2020 turned out not to be quite the knock down I thought it would be. Then came 2021.

The day my first tractor got delivered.

Digging a ½ mile long trench for a water pipeline on my ranch.

Chapter 9

Get Back Up

After 2020 turned out not to be the brutal knock down I expected, 2021 more than made up for it. It was one disaster after another.

One evening, after dinner, my dad got lightheaded, and it didn't pass quickly. We called an ambulance and they took him to the hospital. His blood pressure had spiked into 190s/170s and stayed there for a few hours, then came back down. I've learned that at those blood pressure levels, he is at a very high risk for a heart attack or stroke. They sent him back home without any idea what caused it. Stable blood pressure has long been one of my dad's few good points with his health, so this was a big deal.

A few days later, it happened again in the middle of the day. He stayed home that time. A few days after that, back in the hospital again. We bought a blood pressure monitor for our home to help track whatever was going on.

We eventually realized that it was happening every time he ate even a modest sized serving of anything with carbohydrates or sugars. Natural or processed foods made no difference. One of the 9 trips to the hospital came after he ate half a banana before we figured it out.

One of these hospital trips was from him having excruciating pain in his stomach. That turned out to be a gallbladder blockage. Since the VA took forever to send the blood thinner medicine he needed to be able to have the surgery, I bought it. Actually, the VA never sent it.

While all this was happening and we were waiting for him to have surgery, the fuel pump in my parent's Suburban died. I walked about a mile to get my tractor to tow it home. Then our water heater died.

I said before that my parents were insistent about not taking any money from me. Since they continued to refuse, I offered to buy their Suburban, pickup truck, and some other old parts trucks my dad had acquired over the years. It made sense. Almost all our family's driving is for my business adventures anyway. They sold all their vehicles to my farm company, giving them a little extra money for repairs, and the vehicle repairs were on me now instead of them.

It was good timing. Our air conditioner ruptured next, and that let them afford to replace it.

My dad finally, after a six week wait, got to have his gallbladder surgery. When our neighbor brought him home from the hospital, we had to tell him our well went dry. A third year of a six foot or more drop in the water table had happened after we went fourteen months with no rain. My parents knew the well would go dry in a few years, but they didn't realize that it was happening faster.

After some recovery time, we tested whether my dad could eat carbohydrates or sugars yet. He ate one strawberry and his blood pressure still spiked. It's been over a year and no one has been able to figure it out yet.

Another few weeks after his surgery, my dad and I were driving in what's now my pickup, and the front suddenly collapsed. I got out and saw that the driver's side front tire was about to fall off. He was able to drive home in first gear, where my brother and I swapped the axle off a parts truck.

It didn't stop there. More repairs kept being needed. Some things still aren't fixed. But it wasn't as bad as it could have been, and a few good things happened too.

When my rabbitry got shut down the first time, we had our well pump die. While getting it replaced, the guy replacing it measured our water. That's why my parents thought they had a few years left. He had said it should last until about

2025. My dad took a small loan to get the pump replaced, and borrowed a little extra to build us a backup water system. He and I built a big wooden rack that holds eighteen fifty-five gallon barrels of water. An RV water pump is set up to push that water to the rest of our house. With my rabbitry downsized, but still raising a few goats at the house, along with my turkeys and some pets, that lasted us about three weeks at a time.

Every three weeks, I would hook up a trailer to our pickup so my dad and I could haul empty barrels to a neighbor's house, fill them up, and bring them home. Sometimes, if my dad wasn't feeling up to driving, I would hook a trailer ball to my tractor and do it myself.

One of the best things that happened that year was my dad getting approved for in-home assisted living. It had been over two years since he could no longer dress or bathe himself without some help. Part of that time was him struggling to accept it and apply for the help. But getting that approved and going was a big relief for us. He still doesn't have the wheelchair accessible house he needs, but we'll take every improvement in his care we can get.

The happiest part of the year came from my farm. My experiment with raising turkeys was an exciting success. Before our well died I bought four incubators, giving me the ability to hatch up to 160 turkeys a month. I didn't try to hatch near that many, but I did raise eighty-three new birds and they did well living out on unirrigated desert with a little bit of hay. This is important to my future goals.

My goats, finally on the full paddock rotation I wanted at my ranch, have thrived off the sage brush. I give them a small snack of hay in the evenings so they'll come to me and let me monitor their health.

It took nine months of hauling water from our neighbor's house before we were able to get our well replaced. As mentally draining as that summer was, I kept reminding myself of two things.

The first was to keep getting back up no matter how many times life knocked me down. That became even more important as my dad's health and abilities declined, because he can't fully get back up anymore.

The other thing constantly on my mind was my future. Not just my own future as an individual, but the future of where I live. I had done a lot of studying since my well driller taught me about the constant drop in our aquifer. I learned a lot about the environment in the Great Basin Desert in general. The future being left for my generation and my future kids isn't promising, and I hope to be a part of fixing that.

98

Chapter 10

Different

2021 made me slow down. It gave me a lot of time to think. When we were hauling water from our neighbor's house, I spent the time there thinking or reading. Even when my dad drove me, we both spent more time quietly reading or thinking to ourselves than anything else.

I realized just how different I am. Not better or worse than anyone else. Not smarter or dumber than anyone else. Just different.

Our neighbor's son, Michael, is my age. We've been friends for years. He was who came and helped me make the baseboards and window trim on my house.

Early during summer vacation for him, Michael's grandparents came to visit. That was the third or fourth time I had met his grandparents.

Even though all of my grandparents are sill alive, I don't know any of them. I've met my mom's parents but I was too young when I did to remember them now. My dad's parents have never met me. I can't remember ever talking with any of them on the phone. Same for all of my aunts and all but one uncle.

I don't know if this is good or bad for me. I just know it's one of the things that makes me different. It reminded me of the first time I realized I was a little different.

When I was nine, I had to pay taxes for the first time. I'm being nice if I say that wasn't a fun experience. That was around the same time that news headlines were talking about Amazon making billions one year and owing zero in taxes.

My dad was still on social media back then, and I wasn't yet. He showed me how angry a lot of people were over it. The only thing I was mad about was that I didn't know how to do the same thing for my company. I started studying tax law that day, and corporate tax law eventually became my 5th grade math class.

On the ride to Cub Scouts one time, my friends started talking about what they were doing in school. They were all joking around about having to memorize the names of all the planets in order. Michael said "it's stupid. Like, when will I ever need to know that?"

Then they asked me what I was studying. I started talking about how companies can pay certain expenses, like payroll, in stock, creating paper losses that reduce their taxes and maybe even create net loss carry forward. Wow, the looks I got from everyone. They told me they had no clue what I was talking about. I just shrugged it off and said, "yeah, I'm weird," but I was confused. I still thought back then that they did all the same stuff I did.

Like I said before, it's not that I'm smarter than my friends. I know for certain Michael is way smarter at math than I am. He's smarter at math than a lot of adults are. I study different things than they do, so I think about different things than they do. I think about things in different ways.

I know I'm weird. I'm proud to be weird. There was another time that summer made me think about being different. When I was eleven, near the end of my long summer digging a half mile long trench with my backhoe, the church group for local kids went to a public swimming pool for an end of summer outing. My brother and I both went.

All of my friends and my brother were running around, playing, and having a good time, just like we all usually do together. I wasn't so into it that day. At first I just sat back in an inner tube, floating, and watching everyone else. I spent some of the time thinking about my ranch. Mainly about the fifty-ish acres where no plants grow and how I want to build soil there and plant native seeds like I did around my rabbit barn. But mostly I just watched everyone else, quietly, and enjoyed relaxing.

When I got out of the pool I went and sat with some old people who were sitting at the tables and doing the same thing I was, watching all the other kids play and have fun. I started talking to them and the next thing I knew I had sat there for at least two hours listening to their stories about their families and about the history of where we live.

I occasionally looked over at my friends playing, but I was having more fun listening to these old people tell me what it was like here back in the 1950s and 1960s. I was picturing what that public pool was like before it was a pool. They used to swim there in a natural spring before the pool was built.

My friends had a blast running around, swimming, and playing games. I had a blast time traveling in my mind. We had fun in different ways, and it was a great day for all of us.

If you ever do a search for "homeschool" on Twitter, a lot of the results are all about how different homeschool kids are. It's either public school advocates that think all homeschool kids are friendless, weirdo, freaks, or homeschool advocates who want their kids to be different from all the evil stuff in today's culture. A lot of it gets really mean and hateful. Almost all of it is made out to be negative.

I don't understand why we don't encourage being different as a good thing. Michael and I aren't the same. He works numbers through his head like magic but doesn't understand much of anything about business. I'm constantly looking at businesses and farms to see if I can find ways they can improve what they're doing, but I rely on a calculator a lot more than I'd like to. We're different people with different skills and different interests. That's a good thing. We're supposed to be different.

The times Michael and I talked during that summer I was hauling water, our minds were in totally different places. He was enjoying his summer vacation and didn't want to think about learning at all. Soccer was most of what he talked about. My mind was somewhere else.

Honestly, my mind was a hundred and forty feet below my feet. That's about where the water table was at that time. Learning what I did from our well driller, dealing with my third dry well in two years, and being at his house to haul water, it was impossible not to think about it.

It's just another way that I was different because my experiences and what I learned was different.

Most of when I was hauling water during 2021, and even a lot of the time I wasn't, I spent time alone, focused on embracing being different. Being different is just a tool that we have to help us achieve whatever goals we set for ourselves. And my experiences have helped me set some very different goals for my future.

I had enough in my mind that I had to start writing about it.

Chapter 11

The Future

From my parent's house or my ranch I can see as far as the mountains will let me in every direction. It's one of the things about living in the Great Basin Desert that I love. The views go on for miles and miles. That's about twelve miles in most directions, and over twenty in some.

It made me curious, when our well driller said the aquifer drops three to six feet every year. Our aquifer covers the entire 3,000-plus square mile basin I live in within the Great Basin Desert. One of the things I learned about living in a basin is that the water can only leave by evaporation. There are no rivers or creeks for rain or snow melt to drain into. It either soaks into the ground or it evaporates.

I was shocked when I read that about thirty billion gallons of water gets pumped out of the ground for irrigation every year. I knew it was a lot, but never thought it was that much. I also learned that about ten billion gallons of that doesn't get replenished by nature. The aquifer is being overdrawn by ten billion gallons a year to grow hay. Much of that hay is for shipping animal feed to Asia and the Middle East. And our basin isn't the only one in the Great Basin Desert that has this problem.

I figured surely there are some adults working on this and coming up with some good solutions. I figured wrong.

The government brought a proposed solution that terrified everybody. Just shut down a third of all the farms. Bankrupt farm families, put hundreds of people out of work, and fallow about 8,000 acres of desert. That would take about 72 million pounds of animal feed a year out of our food supply chains. And that's just for this small part of the Great Basin Desert.

A lot of people, especially those that don't live in the rural desert, think leaving the land to be reclaimed by nature is a good thing. It is not. I've dragged my dad around, getting him to drive me to different fallowed fields to look at them. Only one of all the fields I looked at was recovering, and it's on the slope of a mountain, giving it extra water from runoff when it rains.

Hay farming depletes the topsoil. Fallowing a field here has one guaranteed outcome. It creates dust storms that blow away any remaining topsoil. Most of these fallow fields will remain a dust bowl for decades. Even the fields that get some weeds established will still cause dust storms, and much of the weed cover can be blown away in a severe spring windstorm.

That's what happened with the 458 acres across the street from my ranch. Russian Thistle (tumbleweed) was finally taking hold there to hold the soil down some after twelve years fallowed. I can remember dust storms from it so thick that I couldn't go out to feed my rabbits when I was younger. It would blanket everything as far as I could see. Most of the tumbleweed got ripped out in a single day as I was writing this book. That's one set of fields 1/18th of the size of what they're talking about shutting down.

Another forty acre fallowed field I checked has been abandoned back to nature for over seventy years. You can see it on the back cover of this book. It's surrounded by untouched land covered in a variety of natural, native plants and wildlife. But the abandoned land is still barren, just like the 458 acre field by my ranch.

I'm not against re-wilding some land, but out here, human intervention messed it up, and human intervention is needed to fix it. The field behind me on the front cover of this book used to be covered in tall, thick sagebrush, just like my ranch next to it. It was fallowed back to nature forty years ago. It produces nothing but tumbleweed and dust storms.

To make matters worse, desert cities are constantly coming up with plans to pump water from rural areas to their fast growing populations so people can water their yards and pay higher property taxes. Environmental lawsuits have held them off so far, but it isn't going to stop.

And if cities aren't the future water challenge, foreign buyers like China, Saudi Arabia, or an industrial multinational corporation will be. They're already buying up desert hay farms, paying prices way higher than what most aspiring farmers could ever dream of.

Thankfully the government's plan isn't happening. Well, not entirely. The farmers all got together and came up with an alternative idea. Do the same thing, but slower and in a way that doesn't bankrupt them. Slower means still depleting about 600 billion more gallons from the aquifer and dropping the water table by up to 360 feet. And they still plan to fallow the same thousands of acres into dust bowls. But the farmer's plan has an exit I paid close attention to. If *anything* happens to bring the aquifer back into balance, they can stop shutting down production. I have an idea to be that anything.

I'm "just a kid," right? What can I think of that experienced farmers and government water specialists can't?

This is why my biography mattered to me enough to write this. I've grown up right on the edge of these hay farms, but not in them. And I've grown up here studying thinkers and problem solvers who are famous for finding economical solutions. When my friends were memorizing planet names and state capitols I was studying business structures and tax laws. It's given me a perspective that's just different enough that I think I know a way to solve it. I developed a plan I call Great Basin Green that reimagines the products, process, and business structure used to produce food here.

Phase One of my Great Basin Green Plan is buying farms from retiring Gen-X and Boomer farmers before the chance to change them is lost. If they sell to a foreign country or industrial farm, there probably won't be another chance to fix it. I've done the research and have 3 target farms spread across six properties covering almost 7,000 acres I want to start with.

By converting these farms from hay exports to local meat sales, and using the thirteen low-water plants I've studied and used on my farm, I would reduce groundwater use by almost a billion gallons a year. That's 10% of the aquifer's overdraw.

Each field I can convert not only reduces groundwater depletion by up to 100 million gallons per year, it conserves several natural resources. One hay field requires nearly 900 gallons of diesel fuel per year to run. Without having to cut and bale hay, that diesel use almost entirely goes away. And on top of that, these fields each currently require between 175 and 240 mwh of electricity. Watering low-water plants reduces this by about two-thirds, saving as much power as removing around ten average American households from the grid. Fertilizer use also goes away, and I won't be shipping hay 8,000 miles across the globe.

The rest of Phase One is repurposing huge hay sheds into on-farm processing for all farm products, and setting up an employee ownership structure so generational loss of the progress made isn't a problem again in the future.

Phase Two is setting up water harvesting earthworks to get more rainwater in the ground. It's bad enough that the desert gets so little rain. It's worse that we let 80% of it evaporate away.

One of my older neighbors likes telling me to slow down and just enjoy being a kid. Unfortunately, I don't think that's an option. The first shutdowns, fallowing more than 800 acres, is scheduled to happen when I'm twenty-two years old. That's after depleting another eighty billion gallons of groundwater. Then they'll keep fallowing more land, while further depleting the aquifer, throughout my adult life.

I want to raise my own kids here one day. I want my kids to enjoy watching the wild rabbits, deer, and pronghorn that live here. I want them to look forward to seeing bald eagles migrate in and live here every winter, just like I do. That can't happen if we're doubling the potential dust storms every few years and draining the aquifer too deep for regular families to afford water wells.

In part of learning from other people's experience to get a head start, I think of this project while remembering Mr. Buffett's lessons in investing. Early in his career, Mr. Buffett would go for any investment with value, even if that meant extracting value for his investors. Later in his career, he learned that the better path was to grow value, not extract it.

Right now, extraction is what hay farms do. Extract water, extract soil nutrients, and ship hay around the world. Growing value in farming means building soil, conserving water, and raising animals naturally. But using that successfully means using another of Mr. Buffett's lessons too.

Taking from where he said he likes "companies which buy a commodity and sell a brand," fixing desert farming requires producing commodities and selling brands. I can do this.

I'm crazy, right? A 14 year old kid wanting to earn tens of millions of dollars to buy up thousands of acres of farmland to help avoid an environmental and supply chain disaster? Crazy things bigger than most people think I can do is what I do.

This is what my high school years, and hopefully the rest of my life, will be dedicated to. I'm using what I've learned about business during my 1st - 8th grade unschooled years to earn the money I need to fix a gigantic problem.

Right now, a homeschool kid that wants to be an illustrator is working on ten children's stories I wrote to help teach other kids some of my favorite lessons in business. Of course, any sales of this book about my life will help too.

While partnering with a ghostwriter to help me write this autobiography, I wrote a feature length movie about two teens working together to survive the aftermath of an all out nuclear war. It's set on my ranch and is in pre-production planning.

I may be expanding into content-based businesses to grow my earnings, but I'll never turn my back on farming. I've registered a domain to create and launch my own brand of goat's milk based soaps and desert sage products. I'm on track to launch that new business later this summer.

As wild as it is to have done enough unique things by age 14 to be able to write an autobiography, the truth is, I'm still just getting started.

Printed in Great Britain
by Amazon